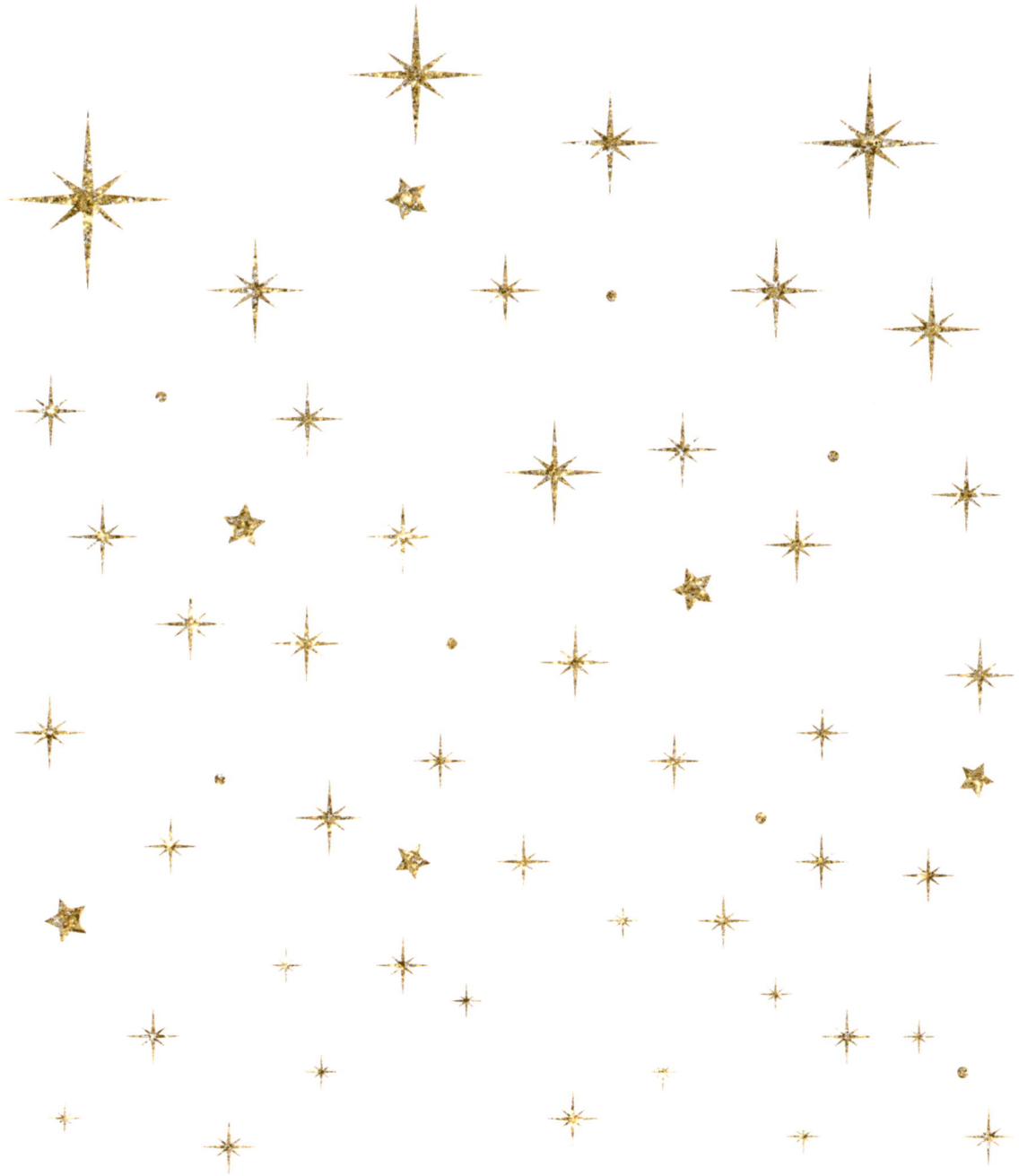

# The Star of Hope

## Tales under the Baobab Tree: Magical Stories from Mama Evie

Written & Illustrated by
Ifeoma Scott-Emuakpor

For my precious daughters,

Charlee-Anne Okiremute and Aimee Emuoboroghene Ifeoma Scott-Emuakpor,

May you always know how deeply you are loved and how brightly you shine in my life. This book is for you and for all the children that read this, a reminder that you have endless courage, beauty, and strength within you. Dream big, stay curious, and never stop believing in the wonder of who you are.

With all my love, always

For permissions or inquiries, contact: info@etherealessence.co.uk

ISBN: 9780576873444

Published in 2024

Published by Ethereal Essence

EtherealEssence.co.uk

It was a cool December evening in the village, and the baobab tree stood adorned with strings of bright paper stars made by the children. Beneath its sprawling branches, a warm glow from lanterns cast dancing shadows.

The scent of roasted corn and freshly baked bread filled the air as families gathered for the Christmas celebration. Laughter and chatter echoed through the village square, but the children's voices grew hushed as Mama Evie settled onto her favourite stone seat beneath the tree.

"Come, children," Mama Evie beckoned, her voice like a gentle melody. "Tonight, I have a special Christmas story to share. It's about a little star and the most important night in history."

The children eagerly gathered closer, their eyes reflecting the light of the lanterns. Mama Evie folded her hands in her lap and began

"Long ago, before the first Christmas, the stars in the heavens twinkled with excitement. They had heard that God's plan was about to unfold — a plan that would change the world forever.

"God is sending His Son to the earth," one star said, her light shimmering with joy. "The Saviour will be born as a baby, bringing peace, hope, and love to everyone."

The stars were filled with wonder, but then came the announcement that made them sparkle even brighter.

"God needs a star," said an angel who had come to deliver the message. "A star to shine above the place where the baby will be born, guiding the shepherds and wise men to Him. Who will it be?"

At once, the stars began to shine even brighter, each hoping to be chosen.

"I am the brightest star," declared one boldly, his light blazing across the sky. "Surely, I am the best choice to honour the King."

"I am the largest," said another, her light spreading far and wide. "No one can miss me. I will light the way like no other."

But among the stars was a small, quiet star who stayed at the edge of the gathering. She didn't speak or try to outshine the others. Her light was soft and gentle, and she often wondered if anyone even noticed her at all.

"I am not bright or big," she thought to herself, "but I am happy to shine in my own little way."
God, who sees all things, looked at the stars and smiled. He chose the little star.

"Me?" the little star whispered when she heard her name.

"Yes, you," God said gently. "Your heart is humble, and your light is perfect for this special night. You will shine not for yourself, but to lead others to the greatest gift of all."

The little star trembled with joy and a little nervousness. She wanted to do her very best, not for her own glory, but to honour God and point the way to the Saviour.

On the night Jesus was born in Bethlehem, the world was still and quiet. Shepherds watched over their flocks on the hillsides, unaware of the miracle taking place nearby.

The little star took her place in the sky, shining as brightly as she could. Her light was soft yet powerful, reaching down to the stable where the baby lay. It was not as blinding as the larger stars, but it had a warmth and peace that drew all who saw it.

The shepherds looked up in wonder, and soon they were visited by an angel who said, "Do not be afraid. I bring you good news of great joy! Today, in the town of David, a Saviour has been born to you. He is Christ the Lord."

The shepherds followed the light of the little star, their hearts filled with hope and joy. Far away, three wise men also saw the star and set out on their journey, bringing gifts of gold, frankincense, and myrrh to honour the newborn King.

The little star felt humbled and grateful as she realised her light was helping others find their way to the Saviour. She wasn't the brightest or the largest, but her purpose was clear, and her heart was full.

Mama Evie paused, letting the children reflect. Then she spoke softly. "Do you see, my little ones, how God chose the smallest, most humble star to carry out such an important task? That little star reminds us of the true meaning of Christmas."

One child raised her hand. "Mama Evie, what is the true meaning of Christmas?"

Mama Evie smiled warmly. "Christmas is about God's love for us. He sent Jesus, His Son, to be our Saviour, bringing hope, peace, and joy to the world. Just like the little star, each of us has a special purpose. We don't have to be the biggest or the best; we just need to let God's light shine through us."

The children sat quietly, imagining the little star shining over Bethlehem. One little boy, who often felt shy and unnoticed, whispered, "Mama Evie, can we all shine like the little star?"

"Of course," Mama Evie replied, her eyes twinkling. "When we show kindness to others, when we forgive, when we share, and when we love as Jesus taught us, we become like little stars, pointing others to God's love. Remember, even the smallest light can brighten the darkest night."

As the children walked home under the starlit sky, they looked up, searching for the brightest star. They couldn't help but imagine it was the little star from Mama Evie's story, still shining to remind the world of the hope and love of Christmas.

That year, the village glowed brighter than ever as the children, inspired by Mama Evie's tale, carried the light of the little star in their hearts. They shared their smiles, helped their neighbours, and celebrated the joy of Jesus' birth with love and gratitude.

This story teaches us that no matter how small or ordinary we may feel, we each have a light to shine. Just as the little star guided others to Jesus, we can let the light of Christ shine through us by living with love, kindness, and humility. After all, "Let your light shine before others, that they may see your good deeds and glorify your Father in heaven" (Matthew 5:16).

www.ingramcontent.com/pod-product-compliance
Lightning Source LLC
Chambersburg PA
CBRC091801090426
42811CB00021B/1903